The Beauties Self-Esteem / Self-Awareness WorkBook For Children K-8

Self Love Is The BEST Love, Give yourself what you deserve which is Greatness, this workbook will teach you how. This workbook has 30 pages filled with amazing activities that will help you with self-esteem and self-awareness don't be afraid to answer questions about yourself that is the only way you will be able to grow into the BEST version of your. If your ready to become a better version of yourself Sign your name below on the line.

This Book Belongs To

....

Table of content

After all Daily journal pages are completed get you a notebook and make your own daily journal. (LETS CONTINUE TO BE GREAT!!)

3 Things
I like about Myself

(1)	
(2)	
(3)	

My Gifts & Talents
What Makes Me Unique?

Small Achievements I Am Proud Of

I Can.....
(a)
(b)
(c)

I Have......
(a)
(b)
(c)

🟥 **T– Is It True?**

🟥 **H–Is It Helpful?**

🟥 **I–Is It Inspiring?**

🟥 **N–Is It Necessary?**

🟥 **K– Is It Kind?**

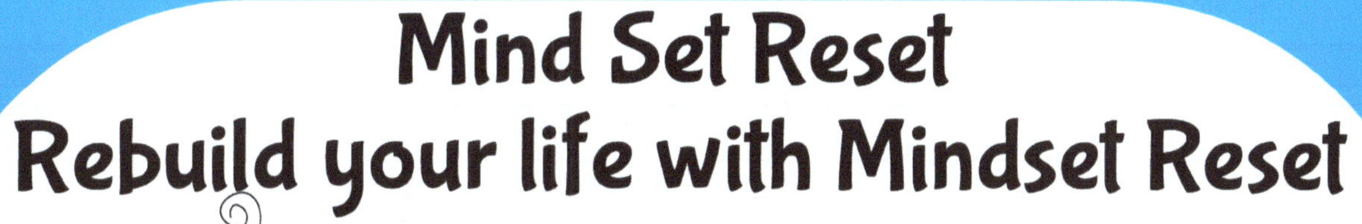

Mind Set Reset
Rebuild your life with Mindset Reset
You are the House

Word Bank

Affirmation

Wealth

Disappointments

Understanding

Hardwork

Negativity

Success

Legacy

Above & Beyond

Control

Gratitude

Fearless

Greatness

Self Love

Dream

Positivity

05

What is Nice Or Mean ?

360 Respect

Draw a Line to the matching word

Hug

Helping

Happy

Sharing

I Love Being Me

What Do You Love About Your Skin?

What Do You Love About Your Hair?

What Do You Love About Your Life?

What Do You Love About Your Name?

What Do You Love About Yourself?

Super Star

1. My name is...........................

2. I am.............years Old.

3. I am a Boy or Girl. Circle one

4. I am a super star because

____

____

5. Draw a picture of yourself.

Be Happy

1. People I Love......

2. What I am Looking forward to?

3. What Makes me smile?

4. Things I am Proud of Myself for?

5. I am Happiest when?

Gratitude with your Attitude

Write A Letter to Someone Letting them know,
How grateful you are for them?

I am truly grateful for

....

....

....

....

....

....

....

Sincerely

....

Hope , Faith & Love

1. I Hope ....

2. I Have Faith In.............

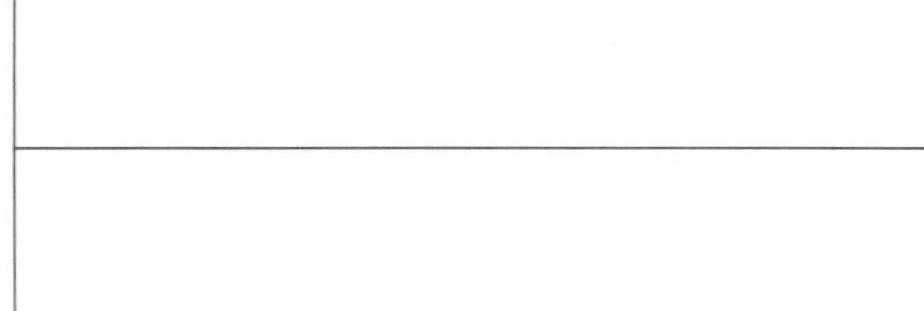

3. I Love............................

Letter To Self

Dear,

I Love You So much..

....

....

....

....

....

....

....

....

Sincerely

Me

SELF-LOVE

(WORD SEARCH)

Find the words listed below and circle them.

W	S	E	L	F	L	O	V	E	C	H	M
O	I	H	U	M	B	L	E	B	E	V	E
R	S	N	B	G	R	A	T	E	F	U	L
T	M	M	N	S	H	E	A	L	I	N	G
H	A	N	V	E	R	I	S	I	N	G	M
Y	R	S	F	I	R	G	N	E	N	R	B
D	T	L	N	G	N	V	I	V	G	N	I
E	G	I	V	I	N	G	E	E	J	G	N
S	J	L	O	V	I	N	G	L	I	N	G

- LOVING
- GIVING
- HEALING
- WINNER
- SELF LOVE
- SMART
- GRATEFUL
- RISING
- WORTHY
- HUMBLE
- BELIEVE
- ME

My Super Powers

I am a SUPERHERO!

Draw a picture of yourself as a superhero

My Superpower is

I use my superpower to

A Letter to My Future Self

Dear Future Self,

Today I am ....years old. My favorite food is ....

I love to ....

My Goal in 10 years is to ....

....

....

Sincerely,

....

write your name

Fill in the Blank

1. I am Worthy of ....

2. I am Grateful for...................................

3. I am Smart and ....

4. I am Thankful for ....

5. I am Strong and ....

6. I Can do anything I put my mind to because I am...................................

Reasons I am Special

Because I can..........	Because I like.........	Because I have.......

Self-Esteem Word Scramble

1. I Get Angry when..

....

2. I like when..

....

3. I feel sad when..

....

4. I Love how I ....

....

5. I Don't Like that I ....

....

6. I Enjoy that I..

....

Like - Don't Like
About myself

10 Things I Like about myself	10 Things I don't Like about myself
1.	1.
2.	2.
3.	3.
4.	4.
5.	5.
6.	6.
7.	7.
8.	8.
9.	9.
10.	10.

Share This with Your Classmates Or Family and talk about why you like them or dislike them?

Mirror Me

What do you see when you look in the mirror?
You will need a mirror for this worksheet.

POSITIVE AFFIRMATIONS

I am.........................

....

....

I will......................

....

....

I can..........................

....

....

My name is

....

I believe.................

....

....

I have........................

....

....

Create Your Own Affirmations to use daily in the Mirror, This will help you Blossom into the Unique Special Person You Are.

CONGRATULATIONS

Awarded to

____

For

Completion Of The Beauties
Self-Esteem / Self-Awareness Workbook

____

The Beauties

MY DAILY
Journal

Today I felt : circle your emotion

happy	sad	angry	excited	silly

Why do I feel this way

3 great things about today

1. _______________

2. _______________

3. _______________

Today I learned

Something I will work on

MY DAILY
Journal

Today I felt : circle your emotion

happy   sad   angry   excited   silly

Why do I feel this way

3 great things about today

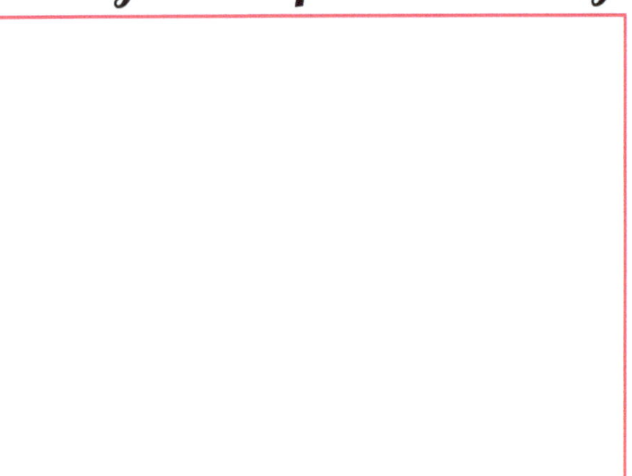

1. _______________

2. _______________

3. _______________

Today I learned

Something I will work on

MY DAILY
Journal

Date: .../..../........

Today I felt : circle your emotion

happy	sad	angry	excited	silly

Why do I feel this way

3 great things about today

1. ________________
2. ________________
3. ________________

Today I learned

Something I will work on

MY DAILY
Journal

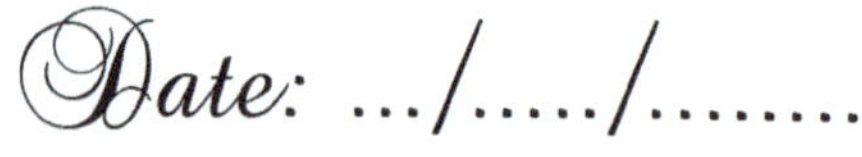 *Date: ..../...../..........*

Today I felt : circle your emotion

happy	*sad*	*angry*	*excited*	*silly*

Why do I feel this way

3 great things about today

1.

2.

3.

Today I learned

Something I will work on

MY DAILY
Journal

Date: ..../...../.........

Today I felt : circle your emotion

happy   sad   angry   excited   silly

Why do I feel this way

3 great things about today

1. ______________________

2. ______________________

3. ______________________

Today I learned

Something I will work on

MY DAILY
Journal

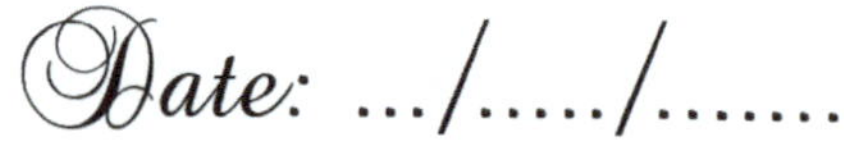

Today I felt : circle your emotion

happy	sad	angry	excited	silly

Why do I feel this way

3 great things about today

1.

2.

3.

Today I learned

Something I will work on

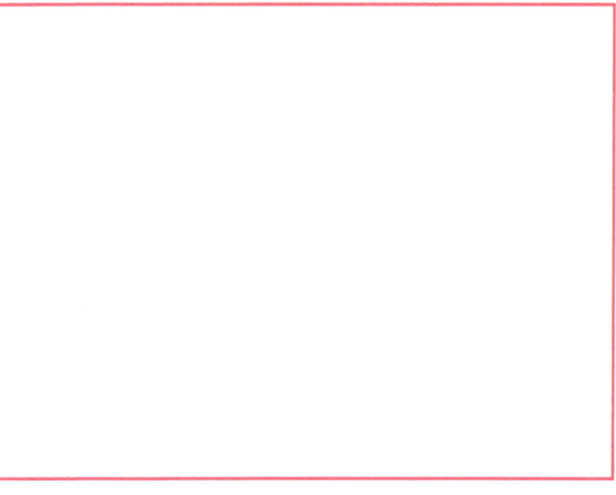